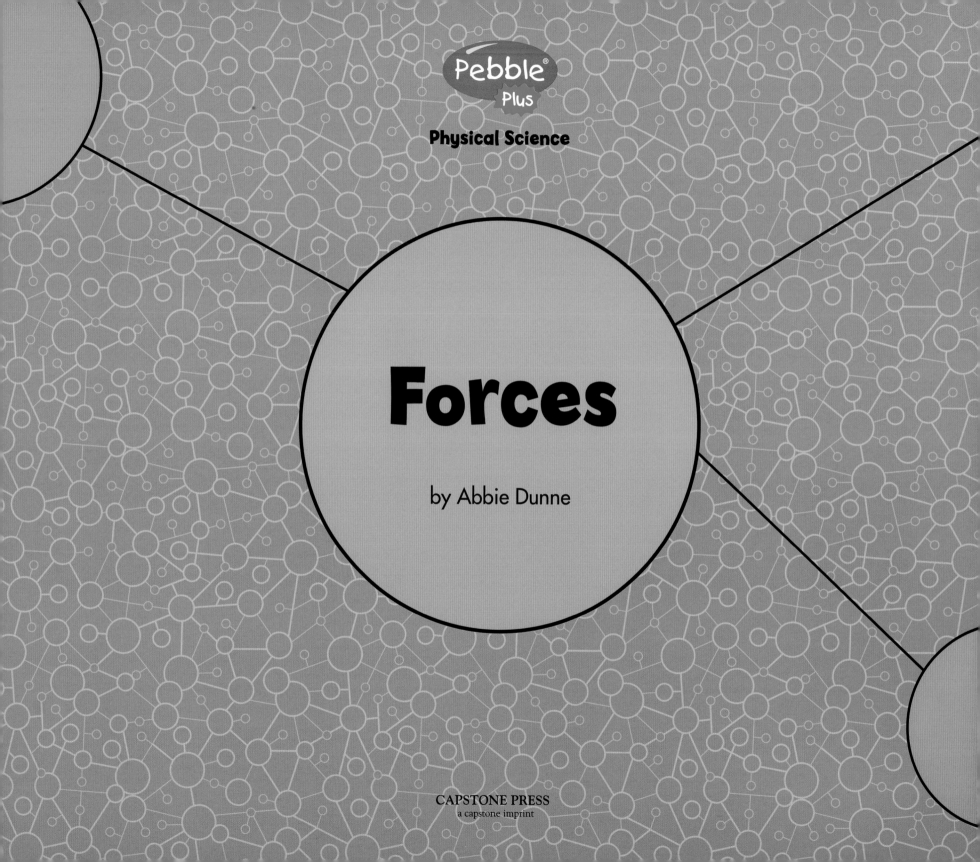

Pebble® Plus

Physical Science

Forces

by Abbie Dunne

CAPSTONE PRESS
a capstone imprint

Pebble Plus is published by Capstone Press,
1710 Roe Crest Drive, North Mankato, Minnesota 56003
www.mycapstone.com

Library of Congress Cataloging-in-Publication Data
Names: Dunne, Abbie, author.
Title: Forces / by Abbie Dunne.
Description: North Mankato, Minnesota : Capstone Press, [2017] | Series:
   Pebble plus. Physical science | Audience: Ages 4-8. | Audience: K to
   grade 3. | Includes bibliographical references and index.
Identifiers: LCCN 2016005339 | ISBN 9781515709367 (library binding) | ISBN
   9781515709688 (pbk.) | ISBN 9781515711032 (ebook (pdf))
Subjects: LCSH: Force and energy—Juvenile literature.
Classification: LCC QC73.4 .D86 2017 | DDC 531.6—dc23
LC record available at http://lccn.loc.gov/2016005339

Editorial Credits
Linda Staniford, editor; Veronica Scott, designer; Eric Gohl, media researcher;
Katy LaVigne, production specialist

Photo Credits
Capstone Studio: Karon Dubke, 17; NASA: EOS Project Science Office/Visible Earth, 13 (earth); Shutterstock: AkeSak, 21, AlexussK, 11, Blend Images, 5, Digital Media Pro, 7, Eric Francis, 19, Fotokostic, 9, Matipon, 13 (moon), Odua Images, cover, Quang Ho, 15

Design Elements: Shutterstock

Note to Parents and Teachers
The Physical Science set supports national curriculum standards for science. This book introduces the concept of forces. The images support early readers in understanding the text. The repetition of words and phrases helps early readers in understanding the text. This book also introduces early readers to subject-specific vocabulary words, which are defined in the Glossary section. Early readers may need assistance to read some words and to use the Table of Contents, Glossary, Read More, Internet Sites, Critical Thinking Using the Common Core, and Index sections of the book.

Printed and bound in China.
007701

Table of Contents

What are Forces?

A force is a push or a pull.
When you pull or push
a wagon, you place a force
on it. The force makes it move.

How Do We Use Forces?

If you give a ball a small
push, it will move slowly.
It won't go very far.
If you give it a big push,
it will move farther and faster.

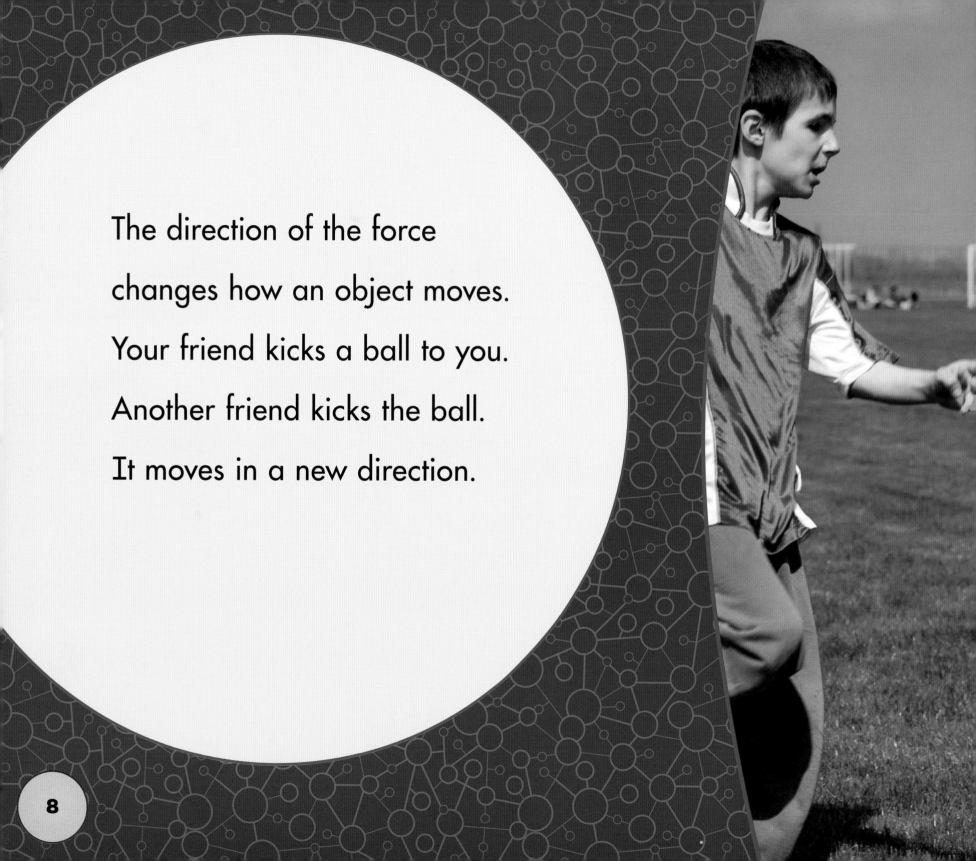

The direction of the force changes how an object moves. Your friend kicks a ball to you. Another friend kicks the ball. It moves in a new direction.

Forces and Motion

If an object is not moving,
a force makes it move.
If an object is moving,
a force stops it. Putting the
brakes on stops a bike.

Gravity

Objects pull on each other
with a force called gravity.
If an object is small,
we don't feel its gravity.
Earth is large. Its gravity
pulls us to the ground.

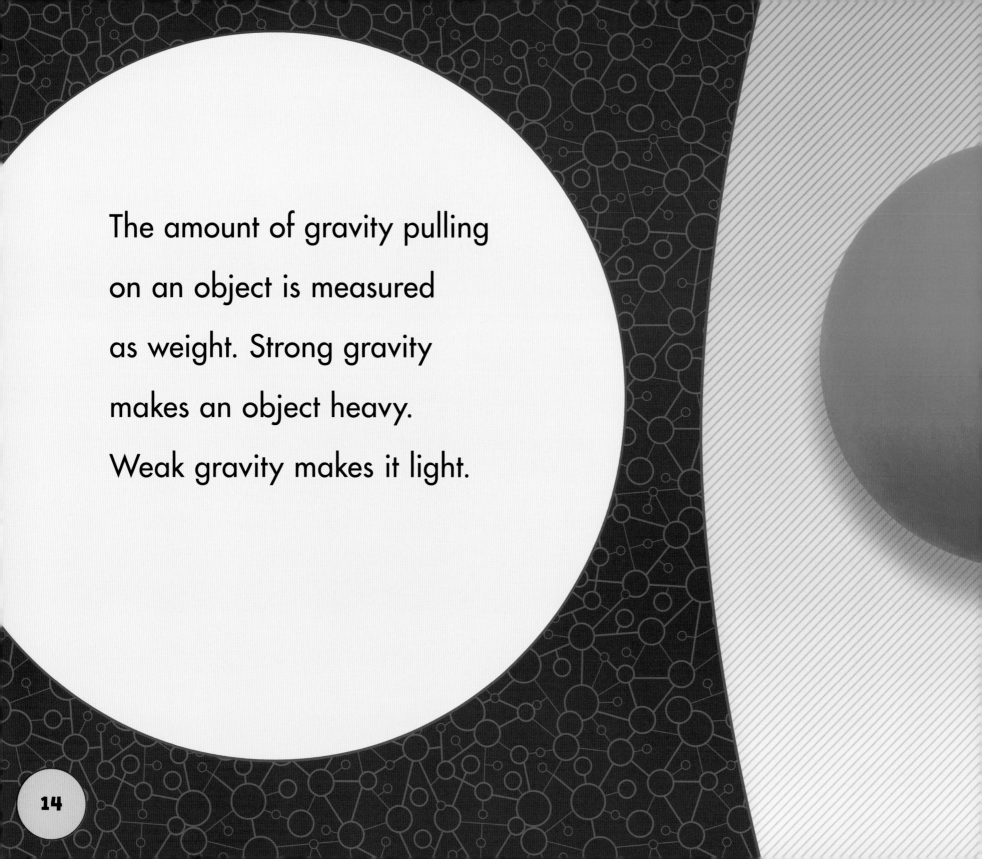

The amount of gravity pulling on an object is measured as weight. Strong gravity makes an object heavy. Weak gravity makes it light.

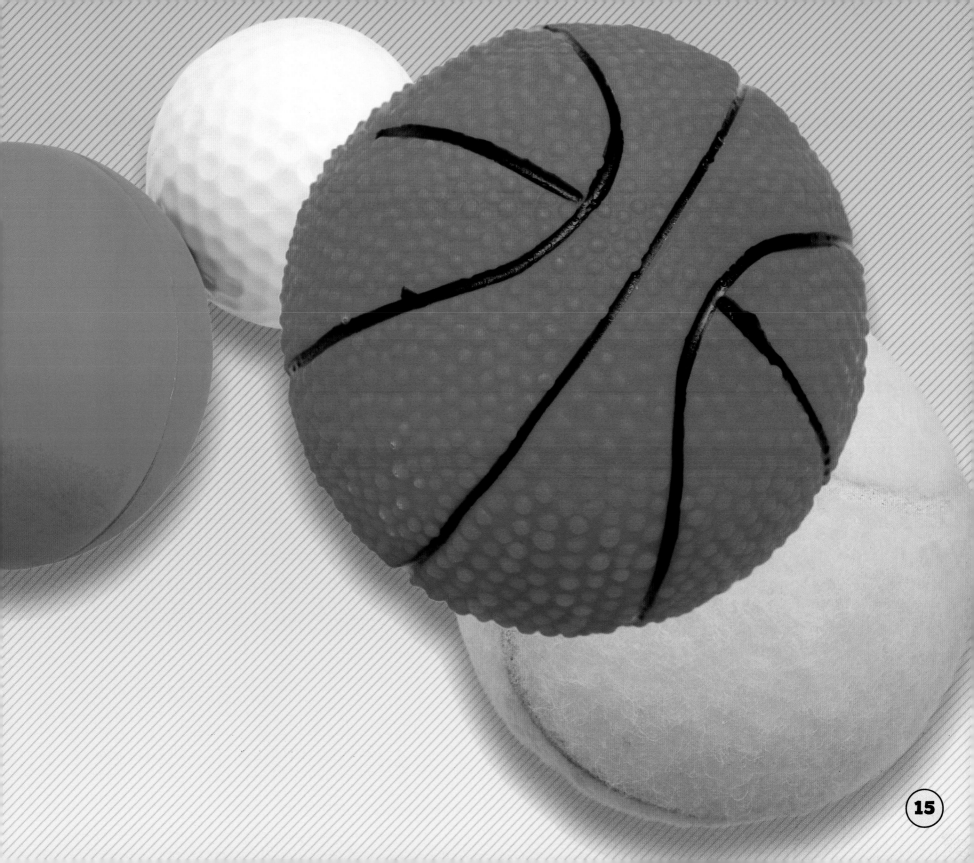

Friction

Friction slows down objects when they rub together. Rough surfaces make more friction than smooth surfaces. It is hard to sled on grass.

Lubricants lessen friction.
Water, oil, and wax
are lubricants. It would be
hard to go down a water slide
if there was no water on it!

Activity

What surfaces create less friction? Guess which surface a toy car will roll farthest on when you push it. Then find out by doing the following experiment.

What You Need

- toy car that is easy to roll

- 4 different flat surfaces on which to roll your car, such as carpet, a hardwood floor, grass, and a wooden deck

- ruler

- cell phone camera or crayons and paper

What You Do

1. Practice pushing the car so that it rolls forward. Practice giving it the same push each time.

2. Give the car the same push on each of the four surfaces. Measure how far the car rolls on each surface.

3. Use the cell phone camera to make a movie of the experiment, or draw a picture of the results.

What Do You Think?

Make a claim.

A claim is something you believe to be true. What type of surface produces the least amount of friction? Use the results of your experiment to support your claim.

Glossary

direction—the way that someone or something is moving

force—push or pull

friction—a force produced when two objects rub against each other; friction slows down objects

gravity—a force that pulls objects together

lubricant—a slippery substance that lets the surfaces of two objects slide over each other easily

motion—movement

pull—to tug something

push—to move something forward in front of you

rough—bumpy; not smooth

smooth—even and free from bumps

Read More

Coupe, Robert. *Force and Motion.* Discovery Education: How It Works. New York: PowerKids Press, 2014.

Royston, Angela. *All About Forces.* All About Science. Chicago: Heinemann Raintree, 2016.

Troupe, Thomas Kingsley. *Are Bowling Balls Bullies?: Learning About Forces and Motion with the Garbage Gang.* The Garbage Gangs Super Science Questions. North Mankato, Minn: Capstone Press, 2016.

Internet Sites

FactHound offers a safe, fun way to find Internet sites related to this book. All of the sites on FactHound have been researched by our staff.

Here's all you do:

Visit *www.facthound.com*

Type in this code: 9781515709367

Check out projects, games and lots more at **www.capstonekids.com**

Critical Thinking Using the Common Core

1. What happens to a ball when you push it?
   (Key Ideas and Details)

2. Name the force that pulls objects toward each other.
   (Key Ideas and Details)

3. If you rub things together, friction makes them hot.
   Can you think of how this could be useful?
   (Integration of Knowledge and Ideas)

Index